HOW & WHY?

INSECTS GROW AND CHANGE

Elaine Pascoe is the author of more than 20 acclaimed children's books on a wide range of subjects.
Dwight Kuhn's scientific expertise and artful eye work together with the camera to capture the awesome wonder of the natural world.

Please visit our web site at: www.garethstevens.com
For a free color catalog describing Gareth Stevens Publishing's list of high-quality books
and multimedia programs, call 1-800-542-2595 or fax your request to (414) 332-3567.

Library of Congress Cataloging-in-Publication Data

Pascoe, Elaine.
 Insects grow and change / by Elaine Pascoe; photographs by Dwight Kuhn. — North American ed.
   p. cm. — (How & why: a springboards into science series)
 Includes bibliographical references and index.
 Summary: Briefly describes how such insects as a praying mantis, silkworm, and bumblebee grow
from eggs and larvae to adults.
  ISBN 0-8368-3009-1 (lib. bdg.)
  1. Insects—Development—Juvenile literature. 2. Insects—Growth—Juvenile literature. [1. Insects—
Development.] I. Kuhn, Dwight, ill. II. Title.
 QL495.5.P37 2002
 595.7—dc21   2001049481

This North American edition first published in 2002 by
Gareth Stevens Publishing
A World Almanac Education Group Company
330 West Olive Street, Suite 100
Milwaukee, WI 53212 USA

First published in the United States in 2000 by Creative Teaching Press, Inc., P.O. Box 2723, Huntington Beach, CA 92647-0723.
Text © 2000 by Elaine Pascoe; photographs © 2000 by Dwight Kuhn. Additional end matter © 2002 by Gareth Stevens, Inc.

Gareth Stevens editor: Mary Dykstra
Gareth Stevens designer: Tammy Gruenewald

Printed in the United States of America

1 2 3 4 5 6 7 8 9 06 05 04 03 02

HOW & WHY?

INSECTS
GROW AND CHANGE

by Elaine Pascoe

photographs by Dwight Kuhn

40280   Insects grow and change

Gareth Stevens Publishing
A WORLD ALMANAC EDUCATION GROUP COMPANY

A potato beetle lays small yellow eggs on a leaf. Potato beetles and all other insects hatch from eggs. Insects grow quickly, and what they look like may change several times before they become adults.

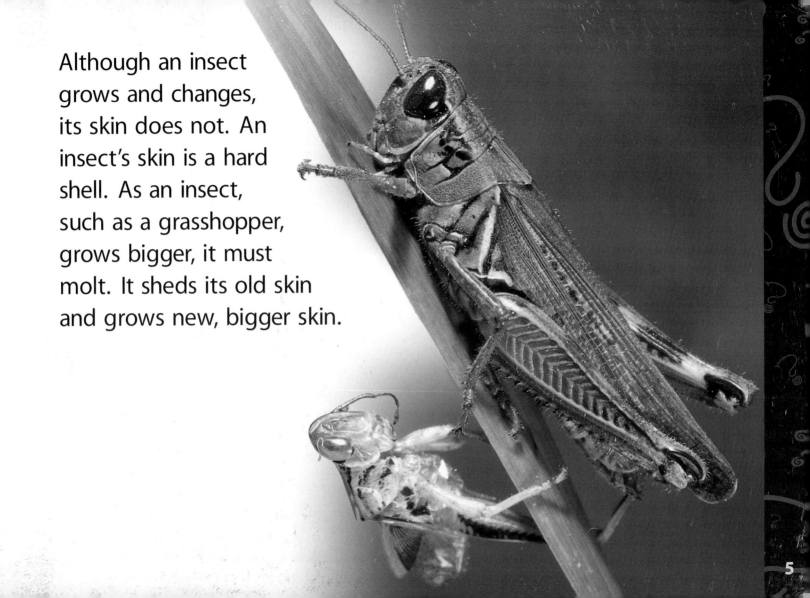

Although an insect
grows and changes,
its skin does not. An
insect's skin is a hard
shell. As an insect,
such as a grasshopper,
grows bigger, it must
molt. It sheds its old skin
and grows new, bigger skin.

Insects such as praying mantises go through three life stages. First, they are eggs. Then, young mantises, called nymphs, hatch. A nymph looks a lot like an adult mantis, but it does not have wings.

As a nymph grows, it molts several times. The last time it molts, it grows wings, and the nymph has become an adult. Growing in three stages, from egg to nymph to adult, is called incomplete metamorphosis. *Metamorphosis* means "change in form."

Dragonflies lay their eggs in water, and the nymphs hatch there. Young dragonflies stay in the water during the first part of their lives. As it grows, a dragonfly nymph molts — as many as fifteen times!

When it is almost full grown, the nymph leaves the water by crawling up the stem of a plant. It molts once more, then spreads its new wings. Adult dragonflies live out of water.

The silk moth goes through four stages on its way to becoming an adult. Growing this way is called complete metamorphosis.

A silk moth begins life as an egg. A caterpillar, or larva, hatches from the egg. The larva eats and grows, molting several times.

When the silk moth larva is full grown, it wraps itself in a silky cocoon, and the larva becomes a pupa.

As the pupa rests inside the cocoon, its body changes to its adult form. After two or three weeks, an adult silk moth finally breaks out of the cocoon.

A bumblebee's eggs rest inside wax cells in its nest. After the larvae hatch, they stay inside these cells. They do not need to crawl out in search of food. Other members of the bee colony collect pollen and nectar from flowers and bring this food back to the nest for the larvae.

As the larvae eat and grow, they change into pupae. Still, they remain inside their wax cells.

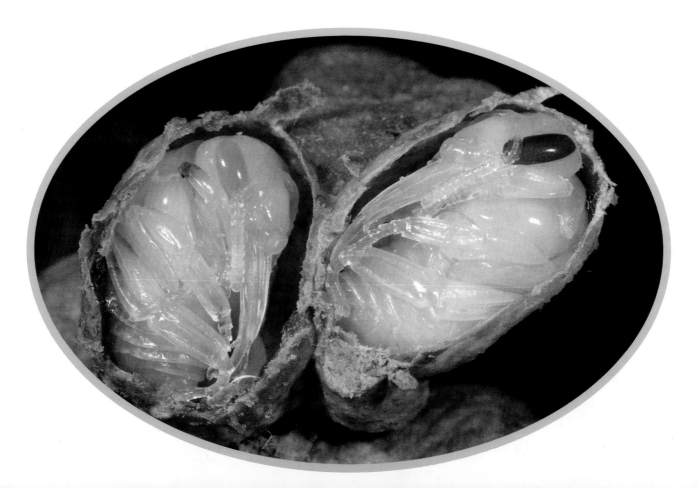

By the time a bumblebee finally comes out of its cell, it is an adult. The bee is gray at first, but its color soon changes to yellow and black.

The bumblebee flies off to a sunflower to gather pollen and nectar. It will bring this food back to the nest to feed other young bees that are growing and changing.

Can you answer these "HOW & WHY" questions?

1. Why do some growing insects molt?

2. How does a young praying mantis look different from an adult?

3. How does a dragonfly nymph leave the water?

4. How does a silk moth begin its life?

5. Why does a silk moth larva wrap itself in a cocoon?

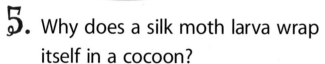

6. Why does an adult bumblebee bring food back to its nest?

(See page 20 for answers.)

ANSWERS

1. As some insects get bigger, they outgrow their hard outer shells, so they must molt, or shed their old skin, and grow new, bigger skin.

2. A young praying mantis, or nymph, looks a lot like an adult mantis, but it does not have wings like an adult mantis has.

3. A dragonfly nymph lives in water for the first stage of its life, then leaves the water by crawling up the stem of a plant.

4. Like all insects, a silk moth begins its life as an egg.

5. When a silk moth caterpillar, or larva, is full grown, it wraps itself in a cocoon for the pupa stage of its life. The pupa stays inside the cocoon for two or three weeks, changing into its adult form.

6. An adult bumblebee brings food back to its nest to feed young bees that are growing in the nest's wax cells.

Dare to Be Different?

Make a chart, with butterflies on one side and moths on the other, listing all of the differences between butterflies and moths at each stage of metamorphosis. In its pupa stage, is a butterfly's protective shell called a cocoon? Do the bodies of adult butterflies and moths look the same? Use library books or the Internet to discover all the differences. Try to find pictures to glue onto your chart to show the differences.

Marvelous Mealworms

Watch metamorphosis in action by raising mealworms, the larva form of certain kinds of beetles. Buy a few mealworms at a pet store. Keep them in a clear plastic or glass container that has oatmeal or bran cereal, a few inches (centimeters) thick, in the bottom of it. Add a small piece of apple or a potato on top of the bran or oatmeal to provide moisture. (Replace the apple or potato if it dries out or gets moldy.) Check the mealworms every day to see if any of the larvae have changed into pupae. To see all the stages of metamorphosis, you will have to take care of your mealworm "farm" for six to eight weeks.

Egg-carton Caterpillars

You can make colorful caterpillars out of a cardboard egg carton. Ask an adult to cut the bottom of the egg carton in half the long way. Paint the bodies of your two "caterpillars" with bright colors, then add pipe-cleaner legs and antennae. Use a black marker to draw on the eyes.

GLOSSARY

cocoon: the silky covering a caterpillar spins to protect itself while it is in the pupa stage of its life cycle, developing into a moth.

hatch: to come, or break, out of an egg.

larva: the wingless, wormlike form of an insect when it first hatches from an egg.

metamorphosis: all of the changes in form that some kinds of animals go through before reaching the form of an adult; a complete change of form that takes place in stages.

molt: to shed an outer covering of skin, fur, or feathers before growing a new one.

nectar: the sweet liquid in flowers that many birds and insects like to drink.

nymph: the form of a young insect that looks like an adult but has not yet fully developed into an adult.

pollen: the powdery yellow grains in flowers that contain male plant cells.

pupa: the stage in an insect's life cycle when the larva is in a protective casing, changing into an adult.

search (n): the act of looking for something or someone in a very careful way.

sheds (v): loses or gets rid of something.

shell: a hard outer covering that protects something inside.

silky: having the soft, smooth, shiny look and feel of silk threads or fabric.

stages: the particular time periods or points of development in an animal's growth.

wax cells: the small, hollow sections or spaces inside a bee's nest, or hive, that are coated with a yellowish wax the bees make.

More Books to Read

Creepy, Crawly Caterpillars. Margery Facklam (Econo-Clad Books)
From Caterpillar to Moth. How Things Grow (series). Jan Kottke (Children's Press)
Ladybug. Life Cycles (series). David M. Schwartz (Gareth Stevens)
A Mealworm's Life. Nature Upclose (series). John Himmelman (Children's Press)
Monarch Butterfly. Life Cycles (series). David M. Schwartz (Gareth Stevens)
The Wonder of Butterflies. Amy Bauman and E. Jaediker Norsgaard (Gareth Stevens)

Videos

Bug City: Incredible Insects. (Schlessinger Media)
GeoKids: Tadpoles, Dragonflies, and the Caterpillar's Big Change. (National Geographic)
The Swallowtail Butterfly/The Mosquito/The Silkworm. (Library Video)

Web Sites

www.fcps.k12.va.us/FlorisES/bugs/preying.html
www.muohio.edu/dragonfly/cycle/
www1.bos.nl/~bijlmakers/entomology/begin.htm

Some web sites stay current longer than others. For additional web sites, use a good search engine to locate the following topics: *insects, larva(e), metamorphosis, nymphs,* and *pupa(e).*

INDEX